The Power of the Word is in your mouth

ROSEMED WARITAY-TULLOCH

CHRIST TEMPLE
LONDON
ENGLAND

Copyright ©2001

All rights reserved.

Designed and printed by CPO, Worthing, West Sussex, England.

Published by Christ Temple, London, England.

ISBN 0-9540133-0 1

Acknowledgement

I acknowledge the power and presence of the Almighty God through His Holy Spirit in enabling me to write this book. All glory and praise belongs to Him alone.

In addition I thank my husband Carl for his love and support, my mother Rev (Dr) Rosamond Jones King for giving me the opportunity to work diligently in the house of the Lord. I thank God for the rest of my family especially Sam, Touffic, Bevis, Saffie, Mariam for believing in me as a vessel of God.

Finally I acknowledge the love and respect of the members of the Holy Spirit Divine Ministries in London.

Preface

This book is dedicated to my wonderful children Zena and Joshua. I realised the power of the Word of God through the many trials that the devil brought to try and interrupt the destinies of my children. These trials have taught me the importance of trusting God's promises and standing and waiting on Him to move on my behalf. God is faithful. If you learn to study the Word, you will learn to trust God and hold firm that HE IS A GOD WHO NEVER LIES (Numbers 23:19).

There are many believers who are not experiencing the power of God in their lives because there is no trust and faith. The Bible declares that the faith of a mustard seed can move obstacles (Matthew 17:20) in our lives. Jesus did not say God would move the mountains. If you have faith in the ability of He that is inside you, YOU SHALL SAY MOVE and IT SHALL MOVE. Faith is your voice of authority. Jesus always spoke the end results directly to the problem and not the present circumstances. The Lord taught me that my prayers and confessions must be the same otherwise I will create situations that I do not want to happen. Never believe what you see, only believe the desired results.

Christians must learn to use their words more effectively because words are a very powerful tool. Words spoken in our lives and over our families either release blessing or put us in bondage. Too many Christians are not receiving from the Lord because the words confessed defeat us. Sometimes we are embarrassed to declare what we feel inside for the fear of appearing different to the world. But we, as the Body of Christ must realise that words are controlled in the spiritual realm by the Word of God. But the devil himself uses these words against us. Therefore the words of our mouths must be chosen carefully and accurately. Only confess what you want to happen. Pray the things you desire and it brings God into your situation so that your joy can be full.

Prayer works with faith. Prayer without faith is void and will not work. Always remember that it was the powerful Word of God that created light when there was darkness upon the earth. The same creative power that is in God is in us because He created us in His image. As you read the confessions, believe in your heart that it will come to pass. Hold fast on to your confession until it comes to pass. The body of Christ must stop walking by sight and start walking by faith. These words were an inspiration by the Holy Spirit and I believe that as you confess, so the manifestations will take place in JESUS NAME.

Contents

Confessions

Barrenness in child Bearing

Key Scripture

"Lo children are an heritage of the Lord: and the fruit of the womb is His reward". Psalm 127:3

I BELIEVE AND CONFESS that God created me in perfection to have children. My body is perfectly and fearfully made. Therefore I will conceive and have children. Father, you declared to Adam and Eve to be fruitful and multiply, I will have children because barrenness is not of the Lord.

Therefore I curse the root of barrenness and break it in Jesus name. I reject every work of the enemy against my womb and cleanse the physical and spiritual womb with the blood of Jesus. My womb is healed because I serve a healing God.

Body, I speak to you in Jesus name that you will come into agreement with the Word of God. You will function in perfection. Womb be fertilized in the name of Jesus and the egg will attach unto the womb for nine months without any hinderance.

Father, at the time of delivery, you shall choose the medical staff and give them wisdom how to bring forth the child. It shall be a quick delivery and painless like the Hebrew women of old.

I will give birth to a healthy child and dedicate this child to the Lord. My child is a heritage of the Lord and shall serve the Lord all the days of his/her life. Amen.

Boldness

Key Scripture

"Have I not commanded thee? Be strong and of a good courage; be not afraid, neither be thou dismayed: for the Lord thy God is with thee whithersoever thou goest". Joshua 1:9

I N THE NAME OF JESUS, I declare that as Christ has given me the Spirit of boldness, I will walk in it. Christ has made me an overcomer, therefore I shall overcome. Christ is building in me a new person of power, authority and above all love.

I will not receive and believe any more lies from the devil as he is under my feet.

I walk in the newness of life in the spirit of Christ who puts me over and above. I am above every situation and will not allow any gifts of God to lie dormant in me. The Word of God shall continue to break and mould me into the divine plan of God. I am who God says I am and will become what God says I will be. In Jesus name, it shall be established. Amen.

Breaking Witchcraft Spells

Key Scripture

"And the Lord shall deliver me from every evil work, and will preserve me unto his heavenly kingdom to whom be glory for ever and ever. Amen"
2 Timothy 4:18

I SERVE A GOD WHO NEVER FAILS. A God who sees the works of the enemies. I break every incantation, ritual, ceremony, vow, initiation made against me in the mighty name of Jesus. I declare every spell is broken. I command the mighty angels of God to be dispatched now into the enemies camp and bring total destruction upon their works. Every work on their altars must be overturned and rendered inactive by the blood of Jesus.

Angels of war execute the judgement of God upon my enemies. As they rise they must be scattered. The sceptres of the rulers must be destroyed in Jesus name. Every strongman must be bound up in the name of Jesus and tormented with the fire of the Living God.

Whatever works I have participated in willingly in my dreams or otherwise, I reject, cancel and destroy in the name of Jesus. Nothing shall by any means hurt me as I dwell in the secret place of the Most High God. The Lord is my Shield and Buckler. I am free because Jesus came to set me free. I am free indeed.

Children

Key Scripture
"And they said, believe on the Lord Jesus Christ, and thou shalt be saved and thy house". Acts 16:31

F ATHER, I DEDICATE MY CHILDREN TO YOU. I believe and confess that my children shall be taught of the Lord and great shall be the peace and the love of the Lord in them.

No weapon formed against them shall prosper. My children shall dwell in the secret place of the most High God and nothing shall by any means hurt them. If their enemies come against them one way, they shall flee seven ways. So declares the Word of the Lord. Their cup runneth over in the presence of their enemies.

My children's mind shall be stayed on the Lord. They shall love Him with their mind, body, spirit and soul. They shall meditate on the Word of God day and night. The Word shall dwell in their thoughts, words and actions. They shall never depart from the Word of God. The will of the Lord shall be done in their lives. They shall live to exalt the name of the Lord. These words shall be established in their lives in Jesus name. Amen.

Deliverance

Key Scripture

"But the Lord your God ye shall fear; and he shall deliver you out of the hand of all your enemies".
2 Kings 17:39

F ATHER IN HEAVEN .... (name the person) is a captive held bound by satan. I ask for your divine intervention in the life of .... Abba Father you are a man of war who came, through His Son, to set the captives free. Jesus you came so that the works of the devil will be destroyed in the life of .... I command every stronghold in the form of chains, fetters, arrows to be removed and destroyed in the name of Jesus. Satan no longer has a hold over ....

Lord Jesus I ask for mercy for the sins of disobedience committed by .... and for the curses associated with those sins to be removed in the name of Jesus.

.... is covered by the precious blood of the Lamb and .... shall overcome the devil by the blood of Jesus. Greater is Jesus who now lives in .... than the devil who has been removed. Father, I thank you for your assurance of the deliverance of .... and that .... mind shall be transformed and take on the mind of Christ, so that the name of the Lord can be glorified in the life of .... Thank you Jesus. Amen.

Divine Healing

"…I am the God that healeth thee". Exodus 15:26

I BELIEVE AND CONFESS that I serve a God who healeth. God, your Word says that Christ died on the cross to take away my sickness. Through Him I am set free from the curse of the law of sickness. Your Word is like a two edged sword cutting through the disease in my body. I curse every root of sickness with the blood of Jesus. I apply the blood of Jesus to cleanse my body from .... (name the sickness). I am no longer under the bondage of sickness. By the stripes of Jesus I am healed. I am delivered, saith the Lord. I have a perfect body. Father, your word does not return to you void. Therefore I have asked and confessed according to your will, I am healed in the name of Jesus. Amen.

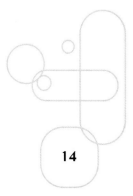

Favour

Key Scripture

"So shalt thou find favour and good understanding in the sight of God and man". Proverbs 3:4

I DECLARE THAT THE FAVOUR OF THE LORD is upon my life. His mighty hand is stretched over my life. I shall be like a green olive tree whose roots shall bear fruits wherever I go. I shall find favour, honour and blessing in every area of my life. The Lord is able to move the hearts of men in my favour so that He can bless me exceedingly abundantly above all that I can ever ask or think. The Spirit of the Living God is upon me and His anointing flows through me and into the hearts of others.

I am an ambassador for Christ and shall receive ambassadorial rights wherever I go. The face of the Lord shines down upon me. I will always give glory, honour and praise for the lovingkindness He has bestowed upon my life. Father, I thank you that you have accomplished your fullness in my life. Amen.

Fear

Key Scripture

"For God has not given us the spirit of fear;
but of power and of love and a sound mind".
2 Timothy 1:7

N THE NAME OF JESUS I believe and confess that God has not given me the spirit of fear. The Lord is on my side and I will not be afraid.

Therefore I reject every work of the enemy of mind control and every other controlling spirits. I declare that every spell is broken. I soak my mind in the blood of Jesus and my mind is free from every shackle of the enemy. I dedicate my mind unto the Lord who has given me perfect peace. My mind shall be stayed on the Lord who has given me perfect peace. I have the mind of Christ which is power, love and a sound mind. God has promised that He will never leave me nor forsake me. Therefore I walk in the newness of life.

My life is in His Hands and God has given me the power to walk in His strength and authority. I believe that I am a new creature in Christ, and I will allow the word of God to take root in my heart, as His word is a lamp unto my feet and a light unto my path. The Lord is faithful and He will establish me. I praise the Lord for achieving perfection in me. Lord, I thank you for making me into your image. Amen.

Finance

Key Scripture

"But thou shalt remember the Lord thy God: for it is He that giveth thee power to get wealth, that He may establish His covenant which He sware unto thy fathers, as it is this day". Deuteronomy 8:18

BELIEVE AND CONFESS that I serve a God who owns all the gold and silver. Therefore as I am made in the express image of God, I claim my inheritance through His Son, Jesus Christ. Your Word declares that I will know no lack as You are my shepherd. El-Shaddai is your name, the all sufficient one. You are more than able to meet every need in my life in abundance.

Lord you have declared in your Word that I am a creator of wealth. I believe that I will possess my possessions in Jesus name. I cover my wealth with the blood of Jesus and command them to locate me now in the name of Jesus.

Every seed that I have sown in the kingdom of God shall yield a bountiful harvest. God shall surrender His best into my life which could be multiplied by a 100, 1,000, 1,000,000.

I shall be called blessed by the nation. Wealth and riches shall be in abundance in my life. I shall be a provider for many and men will see the good works and glorify the Father in heaven. Father I thank you for my inheritance which shall flow now in Jesus name. Amen.

Getting a Visa

Key Scripture

"Therefore I say unto you, what things soever ye desire, when ye pray, believe that ye receive them and ye shall have them". Mark 11:24

BELIEVE AND CONFESS that the Lord will make a way for .... (name the person) to get a visa. The Lord is with .... and .... life is in His hands. .... steps are ordered by the Lord and .... will possess a visa.

No weapon formed against .... receiving a visa shall prosper. The traps of the enemy will be destroyed. The Lord will walk with .... and cut off the plans of the enemies. .... eyes shall see the visa .... and hands shall possess the visa. The favour of the Lord's anointing goes before .... to receive breakthrough and rise above every lie of the devil. .... eyes shall see the visa and possess the visa because nothing is impossible for God. He is a mighty God who is able to raise .... up above .... expectations. Lord I will declare your faithfulness in your house. Amen.

Immigration

Key Scripture

"The earth is the Lord's and the fulness thereof; the world, and they that dwell therein". Psalm 24:1

I BELIEVE THAT THE EARTH belongs to the Lord and every human being that lives in it. Therefore I confess that the Lord has chosen the immigration officers in whom I will find favour. His goodness and mercy follows me. I put my trust in God. The Lord has favoured me with all round blessing and I trust that as the Lord is the lifter up of my head, I will not be put to shame.

I command every mountain of obstacle to be moved in the name of Jesus. Every problem set up by the enemy must bow to the will of God. His will must be done in my life. The Lord has delivered me from the works of the evil one.

He is my shepherd and my passport shall be given the stamp of the land. My heart shall rejoice in the victory that my Lord has granted unto me. The Lord has declared that wherever the soles of my feet tread, he has given unto me. Therefore I have conquered the laws of this land and I claim this land as my home in the name of Jesus. I will bless the Lord at all times because He has answered my prayers in Jesus name. Amen.

Love

Key Scripture

"And this is his commandment, that we should believe on the name of Jesus Christ and love one another, as he gave us commandment". 1 John 3:23

FATHER I ENTER INTO YOUR PRESENCE of unconditional love. I confess that as your love flows from you into me, it shall affect my thoughts, words and actions, so that you will change the lives of people around me. Father make me an instrument of love so that the world will see how great thou art.

Lord Jesus help me to embrace my enemies with love and understanding and to forgive their wicked ways.

I believe and confess that I will walk in God's perfect love which removes fear. I am planted in the love of God and nothing can separate me from the love of Christ. I am a vessel of love and honour. My life overflows with the love of God and His favour follows me in every area of my life. Father, I thank you. Amen.

Marriage

Key Scripture

"For this cause shall a man leave his father and mother, and shall be joined unto his wife, and they two shall be one flesh". Ephesians 5:31

I BELIEVE AND CONFESS that my marriage is sanctified and holy in the sight of God. As God has joined us together we shall remain faithful to each other, love one another, respect, honour and do everything as unto the Lord. We shall be a praying union dedicated unto the Lord. I declare that the will of the Lord shall be accomplished in this marriage. Father, let the fruits of your Spirit of love, joy, peace, longsuffering, gentleness, goodness, faith, meekness, self control flourish in my marriage.

Every weapon formed against my marriage shall not prosper. The hand of the Lord will destroy the works of the enemy. Every mountain of financial difficulties, barrenness set up by the enemy shall be cast into the sea.

I speak the favour of God into this marriage. My God shall perfect this marriage. The anointing upon my children shall increase from generation to generation. My partner and children are vessels of honour, substance and praise to the Almighty God. Father, I pray your unconditional love into my marriage between my partner and myself. I thank you for blessing my marriage and maintaining it. Blessed be the name of the Lord, for He is worthy to be praised and adored in my marriage, in Jesus name I pray. Amen.

Miscarriage

Key Scripture

"Be merciful unto me, O God, be merciful unto me: for my soul trusteth in thee: yea in the shadows of thy wings will I make my refuge, until these calamities are over past". Psalm 57:1

HEAVENLY FATHER, I come to you in my time of anguish and distress. I need your healing balm over my emotions. My heart is fixed on you, O Lord. Extend your mercy unto me as it knows no bounds. My Father and my God, I reach out to you as the woman with the issue of the blood. Let your healing power flow from your river of life, touch and renew me. Your word says that everything that the river touches lives. So let me live in your divine healing, strength and power.

Father, help me not to live in fear of a re-occurence of this event. I believe that it will never happen again. I trust and know that the spirit of fear will not take a hold over my mind. I give my mind, body, spirit and soul unto you. Take me Lord, and lift me into higher heights of blessing and victory. Thank you Father for your overflow in my life, in Jesus name, Amen.

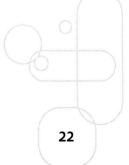

Peace

Key Scripture

"Thou wilt keep him in perfect peace, whose mind is stayed on thee: Because he trusteth in thee".
Isaiah 26:3

EMBRACE JESUS THE PRINCE OF PEACE. His perfect peace overshadows the peace of the world. I receive that peace right now in Jesus name. I believe that the peace of Christ will give me strength and change my home, work, business, children and life.

Every work of the enemy that attempts to rob me of my peace is nullified now by the blood of Jesus.

I cast my cares unto the Lord for He cares for me. I will not worry or fret, but allow the Lord to deal with my future. Lord, you have promised that you will never allow the righteous to be moved. I believe that you are a God who honours His promises as they are life to those who trust in You.

Let your peace, which is like a river, flow unceasingly into my life and be sufficient for me at all times. Father, let my weakness be made perfect in your strength. Amen.

Protection

Key Scripture
"He that dwelleth in the secret place of the most High shall abide under the shadow of the Almighty".
Psalm 91:1

I LIVE IN THE HABITATION OF THE MOST HIGH GOD. He is my refuge and fortress. The blood of Jesus is my buffer zone against the fiery darts of the enemies. God has assigned His angels to build a hedge of protection around me, my home and our possessions. The works of the wicked ones will never permeate God's protection over my life. Lord help me to be vigilant so that the hedge of protection is not broken because of sin.

When I call on the name of the Lord, the enemy flees. Let them be ashamed and confounded that seek after my soul. Let them be turned back and be clothed with shame and cover themselves with their own confusion as with a mantle. Father, darken their eyes to that they cannot see and pour your wrath upon them.

God's truth shall be my shield and buckler. I shall not be afraid of the terror by night nor the arrows of the day. I will rejoice and be glad as the enemy has no hold over me in Jesus name. The Lord goeth before me and has fought my battles as the battle is not mine. I declare total victory in the name of Jesus. Amen.

Repentance

Key Scripture

"If we confess our sins, He is just and faithful to forgive us our sins, and to cleanse us from all unrighteousness". 1 John 1:9

FATHER I COME BEFORE YOUR THRONE and ask for mercy for sins of .... (name the sins). You are a God of mercy and a God of second chances. If thou markest iniquities, no one shall stand. I ask for forgiveness according to your loving kindness. I have offended thee O Lord. Father, I truly repent and I will not walk in these trespasses again.

Your Word cleanses me and sanctifies me. Let your blood of forgiveness wash away my sins into your sea of forgetfulness. I receive it in faith.

I thank you God for your unconditional love and mercy that overflows in my life. May I continue to abide in it and may it keep me from all unfruitful works. Let me walk in the newness of a spirit filled life. I thank you for nailing my transgressions to the cross, in Jesus name I pray. Amen.

Singles

Key Scripture

"Therefore I say unto you, what things soever ye desire, when ye pray, believe that ye receive them, and ye shall have them". Mark 11:24

FATHER I BELIEVE that in your Son's name that I will find the perfect partner. I shall have a spirit filled partner who will obey your word and become what your Word says he/she must be. I believe and confess that my partner will have a mind of Christ, walking in the authority given by our Lord and Saviour. He/she will stand complete in Christ. We shall be of one Spirit, the Holy Spirit, one body and one mind.

My partner will honour, love and esteem me. My partner shall be loving, patient, compassionate, faithful in our relationship and finance, being filled with godly wisdom and knowledge.

My partner shall be fruitful and the fruits of the Spirit of joy, peace, longsuffering, gentleness, goodness, faith, meekness, self control shall be part of my partner's character. My partner shall be a blessing all the days of my life and shall always obtain favour of God and man.

Lord I believe that you shall watch over your word to perform it. Thank you Jesus for choosing the right partner for me. Amen.

Steadfastness in the Lord

Key Scripture
"The steadfastness of your faith in Christ".
Colossians 2:5

FATHER I CONFESS YOUR WORD over my spirit man. I believe and confess that my life shall reflect Christ in everything I do. The spirit of excellence is upon me. God's divine plan for my life shall be fulfilled. My heart is fixed on pleasing my Father. I will serve God with diligence and love. The Word will take root in my spirit man and destroy every work of the flesh-like pride, slumber, laziness and every other spirit trying to oppress me. I will overcome these strongholds in the name of Jesus.

It is no longer I that liveth but Christ that liveth in me. The word of the Lord that I shall meditate on day and night shall be a light in my life. I will run and finish the race that has been mapped out for my life. I am a vessel of Christ and will serve Him all the days of my life. Amen.

Victory

Key Scripture

"But thanks be to God, which giveth us the victory through our Lord Jesus Christ". 1 Corinthians 15:57

I SERVE A GOD who has spoken victory in every area of my life. I come against every obstacle in my life in the name of Jesus. I believe and confess that the hand of the rulers of darkness are destroyed now in Jesus name. No plan of the enemy shall gain ground in my life.

I command every barrenness in my life to be turned into joy. Every dry situation in my life, I speak life into you and command you to come alive and work into the plan of God. I believe that as Christ has made me more than a conqueror, I have conquered this problem in Jesus name. The blood of Jesus is over and around my situation and I thank you for giving me the victory. I shall be like an olive tree that prospers and nothing I do will fail. Victory is mine in Jesus name. As I loose victory and success in the supernatural so it takes effect in the physical. Father I thank you for honouring my confession. In Jesus name victory is mine. Amen.

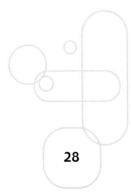

Vision

Key Scripture

"For the vision is yet for an appointed time, but at the end it shall speak, and not lie: though it tarry, wait for it; because it will surely come, it will not tarry". Habakkuk 2:3

CONFESS THAT I SHALL FULFILL the vision set for my life to usher in the coming of Christ. I believe that God's plan for my life shall be manifested and fulfilled. I will always hear and obey the still and quiet voice of God. Nothing shall stop me from accomplishing the will of God. I will pursue the vision regardless of the obstacles I am faced with. I believe the Lord will send people my way who will help me pursue and fulfil the vision.

I confess that the eyes of my understanding shall be opened. Lord, pour your spirit of humility to keep me focused, so that I can fulfil God's plan for my life. I thank God for calling me to affect and change lives in my environment. Amen.

Wisdom

Key Scripture

"If any man lacks wisdom, let him ask of God, that giveth liberally, and upbraideth not; and it shall be given unto him". James 1:5

FATHER I DECLARE that your perfect wisdom which was in Christ should be imparted in me. I ask for the spirit of wisdom and revelation in the knowledge of Christ Jesus. Let the eyes of my understanding be opened so that I may know the hope of my calling in Christ Jesus.

Let no folly pass from my lips. Let the exit of my words to others give light and understanding to the unbelievers and believers. Let your discretion preserve me.

Father, help me to be still and hear your voice. I want my thought, words and actions to be ordered by the Lord. Father, create a perfect mind that will have rest in your will. Let your will be unfolded and fulfilled in my life. Let your Spirit of truth and revelation continue to work our your truths for my part in the kingdom building. Heavenly Father, take me and make me an excellent ambassador for Christ so that your name can be glorified in heaven and on earth. Amen.

Work

Key Scripture

"And he shall be like a tree planted by the rivers of waters, that bringeth forth his fruit in his season; his leaf also shall not wither; and whatsoever he doeth shall prosper". Psalm 1:3

BELIEVE AND CONFESS that the favour of the Lord is upon my life. I believe that at work I am the light that will bring the truth of the gospel to my colleagues. I know that my job/business is covered by the blood of the Lamb. I shall receive promotion, as promotion cometh from my Lord. Jesus will not withhold any good thing from those who diligently seek Him. I confess that I receive a supernatural increase in my wages/business. I shall prosper in everything I do.

The works of the evil one against my job/business shall end today in Jesus name. The enemy cannot harm me as a hedge of protection is around my job/business. I will find favour in the presence of my colleagues. The peace of Christ shall always reign at work. I thank you Lord for the continuous overflow of blessings in my life. I will praise the Lord at all times for the goodness He has bestowed on me. Amen.

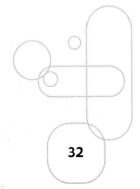